Grasshopping Around Kathmandu

JORGE SAGRERA

Jorge Sagrera

Grasshopping Around Kathmandu

La Pereza Ediciones

Grasshopping Around Kathmandu
© *Jorge Sagrera*

Author contact: jorgesagrera@gmail.com

© Translated by Marc Gandarillas

© Published 2023, La Pereza Ediciones, USA
www.lapereza.net

ISBN: 978-1-6237521-2-5

Diseño de los forros de la colección:
Estudio Sagahón / Leonel Sagahón
www.sagahon.com
Portada y Maquetación Julián Herrera

Grasshopping
Around Kathmandu

JORGE SAGRERA

Translated by Marc Gandarillas

LAZY

And I realizethat every moment in a person's life,when they lose everything,is not an end, but a new beginning.

—Douglas H. Gresham, *Lenten Lands*

A great temple
can be established anywhere.
Because, finally,
the All is everywhere,
and anywhere
may become the seat of power.
Any blade of grass
may assume, in myth, the figure of the savior
and conduct the questing wanderer
into the sanctum sanctorum of his own heart.

—Joseph Campbell, *The Hero with a Thousand Faces*

And I was wondering... Howcould I have lived, for such a long time,alien to naturewithout relating to it?

—Gérard de Nerval, *Aurelia or the Dream and the Life*

ONE

For once, Guillermo decided to walk home on his own. To be precise, he did not really have a choice. On his way home, something got in his way that made him smile—a smile, at last!

He caught sight of a Chihuahua puppy clutching at the legs of two ladies who were chatting on the sidewalk.

"Bye, ladies."

"Have a great day!"

"Bye now, Guillermo!"

The tiny Chihuahua pup began to rub himself against one of the women's calf.

"Leave her alone, Pipo!"

"You heard your owner, Pipo—leave *me* alone!"

Behind his back, Guillermo could overhear the women as they said:

"It seems Pipo's not great at managing his energy levels."

"What would you suggest, then? Should he probably take up painting?"

"If only he could release his energy against your calf—once and for all!"

On the final 200-foot stretch leading up to his house, Guillermo was joined by a playful tiger butterfly. It would actually not be until later that day that he would learn the funny term of *tiger butterfly*, as he googled for some information on the species.

Seemingly, that day the butterfly had popped up from a nearby pine tree. Some days, the insect would like to display a daring attitude, chasing him viciously. On other days, it would just flap past him, in a potential attempt to show him the way. Once, it even dared to land on Guillermo's head, using it as a makeshift airstrip. Oh, that mischievous black-and-yellow butterfly...

"Taxi... Taxi!"

For the second time in a row, Guillermo burst out laughing.

His usual partner at tennis doubles would frequently ask for clarification on Guillermo's unusual ideas and puns. Whenever he tried to explain himself, though, he would prove pathetically unsuccessful. As a result, he had given up trying altogether and had decided to just let things flow. If his partner could not understand a pun, the universe may still laugh as well. Or probably not.

One of Guillermo's children had apparently inherited his particular sense of humor.

As he entered the house, the tiger butterfly made sure to make itself at home. As both made their way around some Chinese jasmines, the insect suddenly disappeared from view. At that point, Guillermo thought he would have enjoyed the chance to say

goodbye. Just protocollary farewell. "See you later."
He was not great at goodbyes, though. To that day,
this remained an unresolved issue for him.

After wheeling his bicycle out of the shed so he
could fix a flat tire, the handlebars bumped into the
jasmine shrub and something hit the ground.

What an unexpected surprise! It was the watch
he had lost on Saturday. How did it end up over there?
He picked up the watch fondly. It had been a gift
from the townhall of Felanitx, which had appointed
Guillermo as the town's "distinguished son." To be
fair, he was not actually a son, but rather a *grand*son.
As for *distinguished*—well, let's just let that be.

It was not long before Guillermo realized that the
tiny holes in the strap were somewhat larger than
they were supposed to be. That might have caused
the buckle pin to loosen.

It suddenly dawned on him that it had been
precisely on Saturday that he had trimmed the
jasmine shrub. There it was. Lo and behold!

He was eventually able to fix the bicycle.

As he reentered the house, he could hear the
phone ringing.

"Hello?"

"*Dad?*" a voice replied across the line.

"Who's this?"

"*Dad, it's me. I've been trying to reach you for an hour
now.*"

"Hey, son. I just got inside."

"*You should always take your phone with you.*"

"Why should I? Are you talking about the landline?"

"*What if something were to happen to you?*"

"In that case, I would likely be unable to make a call—don't you think?"

"*Well. Listen—did I, by any chance, leave my insurance card at the house?*"

"Why would you do that?"

"*I mean, not on purpose… Could I have left it there?*"

"I haven't seen anything out of place. Where did you leave it?"

"*I can't seem to remember. I need to get some paperwork done before noon.*"

"You'll find it."

"*What do you mean?*"

"You'll eventually come across it—just keep your eyes open."

"*Alright, Dad. Thanks. Bye.*"

"Wait—I just found that watch from Felanitx."

"*Oh. Where was it?*"

"Apparently, it got loose—I must've dropped it while I was trimming the jasmine shrub."

"*I'm glad to hear that. Ok—bye for now, Dad.*"

"Don't worry—I'm sure your card will eventually show up."

"*I hope so. Bye, Dad.*"

TWO

A message popped up on Guillermo's phone. It came from his WhatsApp group of former high-school classmates. After initially considering reading it in the restroom, he eventually decided to leave his cellphone in the living room. He was trying hard to take one thing at a time. Guillermo made himself comfortable on the toilet seat, as he resisted the urge to open the vanity cabinet in search for some potential reading on deodorant specifications, eyedrop applying guidelines, or the various Portuguese-language warnings on the shampoo container—and so on and so forth.

His Reiki instructor had once recommended that he should "take life one thing at a time." He had so far succeeded in being compliant. Or, at the very least, he had tried his best—not so much for engaging in mindfulness as for sheer pragmatism. In the past, whenever he had attempted to perform more than one duty simultaneously, Guillermo had frequently ended up wearing his tennis shorts inside out. Since he liked to wear loose-fitting attire, he would notice his negligence once on the tennis court, following a series of unsuccessful attempts at putting an extra ball into one of his pockets.

The message he had received involved a stray dog. If he wanted to be regarded as a kind-hearted person, he should be sure to forward it. Otherwise, he should let the sender know so that they could continue their quest for more genuinely caring folks. On his cellphone, Guillermo checked the notification-muting functionality: eight hours, a week, a full year... He then picked the latter option. At the time, leaving the WhatsApp group for good was off the table—such a decision would likely have weighed hard on him.

Guillermo dropped his cellphone on the couch. Due to gravitational force, the device ended up slipping between small and large cushions, like a stream wavering through a mountain.

He then headed to his garden in search for some quiet reading time.

He had picked one of the books by John Berger.

As of lately, Guillermo had been struggling to focus on his writing. Struggling a bit too much, in fact. It had painfully dawned on him that it is art that creates reality—not the other way around.

As Berger would claim, "every narrative eventually relates to war—either in terms of victory or defeat. Poems, on the contrary, move across battlefields regardless of the outcome, as they tend to the wounded and listen to the fierce speeches of the delirious. Poems resemble prayers in the sense that they are intended to bring some sort of peace."

In the past, Guillermo had lived through a vital era of narrating and singing—about sadness, about nostalgia, about unreciprocated romances, about death.

He liked to compare this time of his life to Picasso's so-called "blue period"—except that, for Guillermo, this had gone on for well over three years. Probably, it was just meant to be that way. It most definitely had to be that way. It could not just—just?—be about writing—painting—the pain and sadness that follows the death of a friend.

> With the brightest guests now gone,
> Green furnishings are down,
> As a shadowless light condones
> the black frost on windowpanes.

Or so Berger himself would write in his poem.

For months, he had been finding it challenging to write. Somehow, the video *Sacred Art, Magic and Consciousness* could serve as a token of how sad and mournful his writing could become—but also how prophetic it could be at times. As he soon understood, there was more to writing than getting immersed in the vicious spiral of venting, verifying, and hesitating. The natural redemption that follows the death of a statement was yet to come. A likely reason behind this was that he had chosen not to write about it, thus not *stating* it. The way in which he liked to write about those topics remained far from being a mere outlet—one that would allow for the cleansing of death and demons, so they could eventually get rid of their rust. There are just too many of us for whom it is not a possibility to drag the load of rust throughout our lives.

As he entered the house, Guillermo remained determined to reply to that message. He would first need, however, to call his own cell number from his landline and retrieve the whereabouts of his cell device.

Somehow, he eventually managed to locate the message, which had now been joined by another twenty-two. He then wrote, "It is just a matter of time before a resurfacing occurs."

THREE

Eager to learn more about the mysterious insect—whom he nicknamed as the "penance butterfly"—Guillermo reached for his bedside encyclopedia. According to the handbook, this butterfly species was notorious for its strength, as well as the array of distinctive yellow-and-black stripes on its wings. Female butterflies were typically brown or black, which would remind Guillermo of the appearance of a tiger.

As he would learn, once they have eventually managed to break through their dwellings, caterpillars tend to surface and feed on the eggshell and surrounding leaves.

When the time comes for building a cocoon, they usually go to great lengths to wrap it in a leaf and further secure it by adding a silk layer on top. After settling in the warmth and safety of their newfound homes, larvae will lead a frugal existence, deprived of any food or water. What then begins, however, remains far from a typical hibernation stage. This is the time when the amazing transformation occurs that will eventually turn caterpillars into full-grown butterflies.

With time, an alluring butterfly will emerge from the cocoon which can fly and feed on flower nectar.

"It also likes to show travelers the way," Guillermo added silently.

Most definitely, butterflies were not a novelty in Guillermo's life. It had been many years since he first crossed paths with them. Shortly after his mother died, Guillermo was standing in the garden on a sunny day, his hands jammed into his pockets, when a couple of butterflies emerged, flapping around gracefully. They were as white as fresh snow.

On the days leading up to the encounter, Guillermo could remember borrowing Elisabeth Kübler-Ross' book *On Life After Death* from someone whose identity was now a mystery. On that September afternoon, the insects caught him by surprise as he was thinking about his mother's recent passing. Not too long ago, Guillermo's father had also died. If memory served, that was back in March. A mere seven months stood between the end of the journey for both of Guillermo's parents.

Those puzzling white-gliding fliers had led Guillermo to write a tale, which he decided to entitle *When Butter(f)flies Back*[1]. The account provided a narrative picture, a brief click, on profound nostalgia as experienced by a mother and a grandmother.

Guillermo continued to write for a bit:

---

1   T.N.: Originally in Spanish, *Cuando vuel(v)a la mariposa.*

A late-evening butterfly,
flapping around Talcahuano,
breeze-lifted through the air.
Of trees or flowers in sight,
There are none.
In the Capital, there are no butterflies, my dear.
In the Capital, there are no butterflies, my.
In the Capital, there are no butterflies.
In the Capital, there are no.
In the Capital, there are.
In the Capital, there.
In the Capital.
In the.
On the balconies,
There is not a single flowerpot calling for help.
My late-evening butterfly;
Oh, my long-lost butterfly...

In the past, Guillermo had written other poems like the one above, such as *The Great Watercolorist*.

He was no stranger to the connotations associated with butterflies, as well as their transformative process. The silver-threaded link between butterflies and penance, however, remained a newfound one for him. Such association was not based on the grounds of transformation, but rather along the lines of reparation, compensation, and recovery.

Guillermo could not help but feel like he was playing a part in those tiny miracles. Conveying portrayals. Channeling their energy. He would frequently be overcome—and overwhelmed—by the delightful feeling of having become a witness to the momentous opening of his third eye.

Anyway. He still needed to ask Marco for an update on the whereabouts of his insurance card.

FOUR

Was he possibly growing a third eye? Guillermo no longer felt that he could trust himself much. Still, he clearly recalled that time when he had developed a burning sensation on his forehead. He felt that way for days, as he began to assume that he might just have been climbing the evolutionary ladder.

A monk placed novice Rampa's head between his own knees, as he started to recite a prayer popularly known as *The Third Eye*. As a mentor, he cautioned the novice against the suffering that he would soon be experiencing:

"This will feel a little painful," the monk warned.

Using a pricker, an assistant started to pierce through the novice's forehead. As the tool drilled Rampa's bone, a crack suddenly developed. Somehow, the monk and his assistant managed to insert a tiny wooden wedge into the fresh opening. Suddenly, Rampa's view of the world began to shift. In the mentor's own words, a third eye allowed their carriers to peek into individuals' true selves, as opposed to the way they pretended to be.

On that occasion, Guillermo did not experience any of the symptoms typically associated with forehead trepanation. Instead, he felt some sharp, easily traceable burning. It was not until later that he could identify the reason behind such a funny sensation. In an attempt to fight fatigue, Guillermo had been resorting to an ointment known as *31 Herbal Oil*. He would typically apply it on his forehead, temples, and the back of his neck. In the past, he had credited the use of this remedy with the stinging sensation—Guillermo's very own "third eye."

This time around, however, something seemed to have changed. That is why he decided to pay a visit to his Reiki instructor.

"That *might* just be the case," Malva responded.

She was wearing a purple-and-orange tunic.

"Are you in a rush right now?"

"Not really. I wouldn't say that."

"Would you mind taking a seat so we can discuss this at length?"

"Sure."

At that very moment, the breeze caused the wind chime to jingle.

"How's everything going, by the way?"

"So far, so good."

"It's just a matter of time—you're already aware of that, aren't you?"

The wooden tubes in the chime began to beat the clapper repeatedly, its percussive sounds resembling actual heartbeats.

"Sure I am."

At that point, Guillermo realized that a mantra had been added to the wall: '*The upside of pain is that it leads us to a place where things may be viewed from a different perspective.*'

"Did you write that yourself?"

"Did I write what?"

"That sentence over there," Guillermo responded as he pointed at the wall.

Malva responded, not even feeling the urge to turn around and look at the wall herself.

"I guess I did."

Guillermo stared at the wall for a while, as he ruminated whether Malva might have already grown her third eye.

"What about that tunic you're wearing?"

Reaching over her breasts with the back of her hand, Malva took hold of her tunic, then briskly slid it all the way down.

"Do you like it? I sewed it with my own bare hands."

"That's what I presumed."

"To be honest, all I had to do was cut two old tunics in half, then sew them together."

As she awaited Guillermo's answer to her recent question, Malva began to grow increasingly impatient:

"So, you *like* it or not?"

"Of course I do. It looks like a unique piece."

Malva smiled. Guillermo raised his hand as he began to stretch one of his fingers.

"By the way, do you happen to remember if we went to see *Hair* together?"

"Are you talking about *Hair, The Musical*?"

"That's right."

"I think I never got to see it. Why are you asking?"

"Just look at that dress. There are some New Age-ish vibes to it, don't you think?"

Resembling a moon landing, Malva's hands began to slowly descend onto the Tibetan tapestry covering the table.

"I don't seem to remember who it was that came with me to see that play."

"I guess that must've been back in the 70s, right?"

"I believe that was even earlier than that."

"Back in the day, we really liked to keep crazy busy, didn't we?"

"You got that right. On that day, I remember experiencing some sort of *satori*."

"Ha! You must be kidding."

"I'm not. I can remember something about that woman sitting next to me. I recall holding her hand and feeling my arm start to glow all the way up to my heart."

"Are you sure you're talking about your *arm*? Gosh, you're hilarious!"

"Still, I don't seem to have a recollection of that woman's identity…"

"Have you considered that lady you mention might not have actually been a grown *woman*? Try not to overdo it, Guillermo. Unless I'm mistaken, you must've been around fifteen at the time…"

Malva used her hands to smoothen the Tibetan tapestry. That provided a transient break, yet one that was long enough to allow her to switch gears:

"You were inquiring about your third eye."

"I was."

"Are you keeping up with your practice?"

"I am—not as often as I'd like to, though."

"You need to keep practicing. That's the only path forward."

"I guess you're right."

Guillermo raised the small wooden hammer, causing the metal rod in the pin to reverberate. He took advantage of the prolonged chime in the B note, which allowed him to buy some time.

"You know me well. I tend to get my inspiration from here and there," he said. "I'm not the kind of person that likes to become pigeonholed."

Malva snatched the ball-peened hammer from Guillermo's hands.

"At this point, your best choice remains to avoid any sources of distraction. Your *from-here-and-there* approach to inspiration doesn't come without its downsides."

"Alrighty, then. I'll try to find more time so I can focus on my practice."

"Exactly. That's the best thing you can do."

"On a different note—have you seen Daniela lately?"

"I haven't seen her around. At least not for a while."

"Apparently, she left her yoga mat in here."

"We are both participants in one of those messaging groups."

"Great. Will you make sure to let her know about her mat?"

"Sure, I will. By the way, do you mind if I get some Nag Champa incense?"

Malva took her time to sniff the sticks before handing them over to Guillermo.

"Mmm, *Magnolia Champaca*. One of the best smells out there..."

"How much are those?"

"Never mind—this one's on me."

"Thanks, then. I need to run now. See you soon."

On his way out, Guillermo assisted the wind-chime clapper in pumping a cleft—one that would go straight to the hearer's heart. That was a treble clef, also known as the G clef—the one typically used for high-pitched sounds.

"Bye for now, Guillermo. Take care."

FIVE

uillermo embarked on a quest for some old
pictures that he kept in a cardboard box.
Hopefully, those would help him bridge his
memory gaps, which were becoming increasingly
common. He was therefore searching for his external
memory—his very own flash drive, so to speak. Not
that it was likely for any cameras to have been
around on that day. At any rate, Guillermo decided
to take his time and examine the old pictures and
magazine clippings inside the old box. Among other
memorabilia, Guillermo could find a number of old
tickets to once-in-a-lifetime concerts like those held
by The Carpenters or Chicago—just to name a couple.
And there it was, at long last—his ticket to *Hair, The
Musical!* He put it aside gently. To keep it in view, he
would be using it as a bookmark from then on.

More enthusiastically than ever, Guillermo
resumed his nostalgic search. He even came across
a few pictures from his graduation trip, which had
been taken with a Polaroid. Guillermo sharpened his
eyesight in an attempt to identify those tiny faces.

As immersed as he was in his treasure hunt,
Guillermo overheard the chime that signaled an
incoming message. At this point, it felt like he was

undergoing some sort of synesthesia. As he struggled to keep his eyesight nice and sharp, Guillermo's sense of hearing also appeared to benefit from the whole process. He left the room and headed for the kitchen.

The notification that he had received was related to one of those instant voice messages. In the recording, Daniela was straightforward in her request—was he available for a last-minute meet-up?

Guillermo thought he would take the opportunity to bring along his *Hair, The Musical* ticket. Had he had a say in the matter, though, he would have probably chosen someone other than Daniela to get his heart-side arm awakened on that day.

While Daniela ordered a cup of homemade coffee, Guillermo went instead for a mint-and-ginger lemon juice.

"How're things with you?"

"Everything's fine. Thanks for asking."

It did not take long before their order was ready. For a while, both stayed quiet, apparently unable to take the lead in the conversation. As used as they were to running into each other on social media, it had been a while since they had last met face to face. Anxiously, Daniela checked the watch on her wrist as she informed Guillermo that she would probably have to leave soon. She had planned on eating lunch with her daughter. Visibly pressed for time, Daniela decided to cut to the chase:

"How come you knew about the dog?" she asked.

"What dog are you talking about?"

"The one in the picture from the messaging group."

"Oh. That dog…"

"Yes. *That* dog."

"How's he doing, by the way?"

"I don't have a clue, to be honest."

"So, why would you ask?"

"I was wondering how you could anticipate that he would show up eventually."

"Are you sure that's exactly what you asked?"

"I don't think my original question matters anymore."

At that point, Guillermo decided to update Daniela on his encounter with the tiger butterfly, as well as the enigmatic retrieval of his watch. (As for his insurance card, he did not mention anything yet—he would first need an update himself.)

"Although the odds were not on my side," Guillermo said, "I decided to test-run the dog first, so I made a retrieval wish."

After grabbing a pen from his shirt pocket, Guillermo wrote something on his napkin.

"*Come hell or high water*," Guillermo said, "*the sun is still shining.*"

Daniela rolled her eyes discreetly:

"Is that what you just wrote down?"

"Not really. I wrote a sentence I recently heard from someone on the street: *You cannot give the gift of something that you are yet to try yourself.*"

"Oh well. What would that mean?"

"I'm still trying to figure that out myself..."

"So, why would you write that down?"

"Daniela, I think you shouldn't ask so many questions."

"Okay, then. Listen—getting back to the dog thing..."

"That's the reason why we're here, right?"

"... last night, I dreamed of one of those sightseeing buses you would typically see touring around the Capital."

"Wow."

"It was a yellow bus. In my dream, it was incredibly vivid."

Some people had started to gather at the intersection of the boulevard and the main road.

"Do you have any idea what my dream might actually mean?"

"Do you want me to go ahead and interpret your dream?"

"I'm looking forward to it."

"Well. I'm afraid what I'm about to tell you will probably not make sense..."

"What do you mean?"

"It won't be easy for me to interpret your dream without further context."

"Gotcha."

"Are you dating someone at the moment?"

"What!?"

"Thing is, I'm seeing a baby is on its way."

"How dare you, Guillermo!"

Daniela started to search her purse thoroughly.

"I got this—my treat."

Daniela zipped her purse, looking both confused and somewhat offended.

"I was trying to find my hand-held mirror—to no avail."

A few Saint Francis School students were coming in droves to attend the saint's procession. They were carrying along white-and-yellow balloons, symbolizing the colors of the Vatican flag.

"I can also see some wealth."

"Oh well," she had placed her purse on her lap. "*That* definitely sounds way better!"

"Let me ask you something."

"Go for it."

"Do you remember coming to the theater with me for *Hair, The Musical*?"

"What?"

"I don't seem to remember who was sitting next to me that day."

"On the bus?"

"At the theater."

"Guillermo, the entire group was there that day. We went on a day trip with the association, remember?"

Guillermo began to recall some of the details surrounding that day. Piece by piece, familiar faces started to flood his memory—sometimes slowly and weakly, other times blurrily and anonymously. He recalled traveling on an economy rental bus. It had taken a while before they had eventually reached their destination. The atmosphere inside the bus had not been particularly peaceful, as it would later become apparent at the play. Those on board were returning from a so-called "intertribal" contest, which had featured a fierce competition between two teams—the Onas and the Comanches. Their Physical Education instructor had probably not had the greatest idea when he decided on bringing native Fuegians and Mexican Americans face to face.

"Anyway," Daniela said. "I fail to see how it'd be relevant to retrieve the identity of the person sitting next to you."

"Well, you're probably right. Speaking of which—I never found it easy to pronounce the association's name."

"*Archaeopteryx*."

"Yup. We should probably have picked an easier name, don't you think? Off the top of my head, what about 'The Ninth Cucumber' or 'The Red Knight'? I can clearly remember how, back in the day, saying the association's name aloud would get me drooling every time I tried to sell a raffle ticket to a passer-by."

Daniela and Guillermo had no choice but to cross the street amidst scenes of devotion. One of the children approached Daniela and handed her a yellow balloon. Daniela gave Guillermo an astonished look.

"Did you just see that?" she exclaimed. "Yellow seems to be stalking me these days."

"Ma'am," the child politely said to Daniela in order to draw her attention. "Would you mind if I gave you another two balloons? These are the last two I've got left. I was asked to hand out way too many of those."

Somehow, Daniela and Guillermo managed to escape the crowd just as the believers started to chant a religious hymn.

"By the way, Daniela—Malva told me you forgot your yoga mat at the studio."

"Did I? Speaking of which—what am I supposed to do with these?"

Packed with helium gas, the balloons appeared ready to go and conquer the skies above.

"You may want to give them to your grandson..."

"Great idea—except that I don't seem to have any grandchildren, at least for the time being."

"... Also, you should be mindful..."

"Of what?"

"… that you're holding exactly *three* balloons—not one more, not one less."

"Urgh. Don't make me curse you again, you little bastard! Here you go—they're all yours."

SIX

Guillermo and, now, *his* balloons kept on strolling. At this point, Guillermo realized that he was looking a little flashy. No matter what, he liked to think of himself as being unimpeachable—*and* unpunishable. He was *the* WRITER, in capital letters.

"A *real* writer!"

Even as only a handful of his fellow villagers owned his books (according to his own calculations, as little as 0.01% of the local population), Guillermo was *still* a reputable writer in town.

Amidst such ruminations, Guillermo pushed the dancing balloons away from the bougainvilleas that dotted Del Mar Street. The elongated fuchsia fingers of those bushes appeared to be reaching out for his golden balloons.

He then kept walking down the avenue.

It was October and, as such, the Argentinian spring was dancing on the surface, as a powerful floral scent seemed to originate from the sea.

Even as he was just starting to overcome Iris' loss, Guillermo still had a long way to go prior to attaining a zenithal balance in his life.

Speaking of reaching summits—there it was. Right before his eyes.

He anchored the cords to a nearby rock. The balloons started to wave, resembling beach flags. As those, the balloons seemed to be providing a watchful warning.

"*Poetry*—that's what the balloons must be signaling," Guillermo thought. "Some kind of poetry that remains well within their reach."

> *AVERTISSEMENT*: *Ne laissez pas échapper la poésie*

Using his tiny notepad, Guillermo wrote:

> *There she awaited that final ray of sunshine, all the way till the end.*

On a new sheet, he added:

> *There she stayed until the final light was shot.*

Yet, on a different sheet:

> *There she kept the final blaze, which she pampered… all the way till the end.*

"Iris, my one true love, I wish you enjoyed your ride to your own heaven."

Guillermo tied a knot out of each golden thread. '*Oh, tie a yellow ribbon 'round the old oak tree…*' Those verses were released up in the wind—well beyond the sea.

He then embarked on his return, leaving behind nothing but transient footprints on the sea-moistened soil.

SEVEN

Iris had spared no words to alert Guillermo. With a sigh, she had warned him as she was being surrounded by tiny cracks that provided a glimpse into her glowing ribs. Her delicate Eve-like ribs.

"Remember—rusty sorrows may lurk behind a cheerful jingling bell."

That was the last thing Guillermo could hear from Iris prior to her final departure.

On his journey from the sea, Guillermo had tried to gather a few relevant memories. He would then invite those into his heart as endless recollections kept scrolling the path into his soul. Some of those remembrances appeared to be thoughtful enough to restore the bark that had long fallen off the surrounding poplars...

At this time, however, restoration could not reach fulfillment as Guillermo's phone started to ring insistently.

"*Hey, Guillermo!*" Daniela exclaimed from the other end of the line.

"Hello?" Guillermo answered, almost simultaneously.

"*I'm just about to turn your weekend upside down.*"

She sounded excited—so. very. excited.

"*On my way home, I came across a Spanish playing card that was lying on the ground. No wonder it was covered in mud from the rain. Still, the symbol was perfectly visible. Now, guess what kind of card it was...*"

"Now you're just 'killing me softly,' Ms. Roberta Flack. Just go ahead and 'tell me softly.'"

"*I'm afraid it won't be that easy—you'll have to make a guess!*"

"Please 'tell me softly,' Daniela. I'm not in the mood today, you know."

"*The three golden coins.[2]*"

When she had first seen the card, Daniela had decided not to disrupt Guillermo's weekend. Instead, she had planned to hold her horses until well into the New Year. When she had entered her home, however, Daniela had found her daughter waiting for her. As she continued to tell Guillermo over the phone, it did not take long before she realized there was something going on. She had thought to herself, "*Guillermo's got to be behind this.*" Daniela's daughter, who had started to weep, hugged her mother as she whispered in her ear: "Mom... I'm expecting a baby..."

Daniela's end of the phone suddenly became quiet for a while.

"Daniela, that's such wonderful news. Congratulations!"

---

2   T.N.: Originally in Spanish, el tres de oros.

"It is, indeed! My daughter and her partner have been trying to conceive a child for a while now."

"What about the card?"

"Which one?"

"The playing card you just mentioned."

"Yes. What about it?"

"Did you get to pick it up?"

There was more silence on Daniela's end.

"Goodness gracious... What if I ended up becoming the grandmother of triplets!?"

EIGHT

Guillermo enjoyed picturing himself as Sean Penn in the final scenes of *The Tree of Life*—as a devastated, lost soul in the vastness of the earth. Overwhelmed by a state of total emptiness in terms of the significance of life.

What about Iris? She could have very well played the part of Miss O'Brien: 'Why, sir? Where have you been? Were you aware of this? What do we actually mean to you? Please give me an answer—I'm begging you.'

He was early for his tennis club routines. The weather was not great, so he wanted to check in advance how crosswinds might be affecting his shots that day. He suggested to one of the outcoming coaches that they should practice their shots for a while. Side winds tend to slightly divert the ball from its intended path. Should he choose to move closer to the ground, he thought, that would likely assist in mitigating undesired effects from the wind.

It was right then that Cosme arrived. Together, they had been playing doubles for a year. The sporty couple seemed to complement each other seamlessly. While they were playing ball with some opponents, Guillermo suggested to his partner:

"If you raise your ball that high into the air, you're risking it being swayed away by the wind."

Cosme complied with Guillermo's recommendation. He was the competitive kind. Back in the day, both had once met with grim faces for some junior finals. This time, Guillermo appeared to be more collected. He had probably channeled his libido through unrelated activities—libido, that is, as understood by Jung, as he would later try to explain.

Now, time had come for them to work on their serves.

"Cosme," Guillermo said, "if that's fine with you, I'll treat you later to a glass of Cinzano vermouth—there's something I need to tell you."

"I'm in—especially if we end up winning the match."

Guillermo hit a couple of flat serves.

"We'll win—that's for sure!" Guillermo said, enthusiastically.

The start to the game could not have been smoother. The opponents were apparently set on the usual shots—high and long, reaching all the way out to the boundaries of the tennis court. As the wind whimsically swayed their shots, they started to realize that their attempts were not being particularly well-aimed.

In high spirits, Cosme started to crack a few jokes here and there, not even sparing a few instances of coarseness. After a glorious first set (6-3), he euphorically headed out for a break. He then recalled the story of those Spaniards who, one summer, had made it to the club by boat. As the welcoming hosts that they took pride in being, Cosme and the others had invited the newcomers to play. At one point, one of the Spanish guys uttered a few indistinct words that Cosme understood as:

"You're wrong, my friend."

Cosme was standing next to the net. He would not move—just in case. Although he did not seem excessively concerned about potentially blocking the opponent's view, he still decided to remain friendly. In the end, the Spanish sailors turned out not to be great at tennis. He moved a bit to the right.

Sometime later, after he had again thought that he was getting the "you're wrong, my friend" message, Cosme started to move in any given direction. At that very moment, what seemed to matter most to him was to stop. being. wrong.

Finally, one of the Spanish guys seemingly decided to put an end to the game, as he grabbed the tiny ball, squeezed it into his hands, then started to make it bounce energetically:

"Something's off—this ball's not bouncing the right way."

As he continued his account, Cosme focused on how one of the opponents had twisted his ankle right after the start of the second set.

"It's undoubtedly that we're bound to win."

"It's on purpose that you cooled us down."

Guillermo then headed to the other side of the court and, with the aid of the opponent, carried the injured guy to a nearby chair.

"Would you mind if I tried?"

Guillermo started to apply some Reiki on the doomed player's ankle.

Cosme holstered his racket and put it back inside the bag.

"What do you think you're doing, bud?" the player wondered.

Guillermo was trying to keep his own eyes half closed.

"Just some Reiki," he responded.

"You're laying your hands."

The guy stared at Guillermo from below:

"Wouldn't Jesus also lay his hands?"

"Where would he do that?" Cosme asked.

"On people, as well as on certain items."

"I can't believe we're actually comparing *him* to Jesus."

"Well—what about yourself? Don't you enjoy comparing yourself to Guillermo Vilas from time to time?"

NINE

He could not help but regret having invited him. The injury on the ankle appeared to have healed rather quickly. Still, they decided not to take their chances and stop the match.

"Sure," Cosme said. "That certainly appears to be the safest bet at this point."

Then, they headed to the club's café, where they treated them to some Cinzano vermouth.

Guillermo took this opportunity to update them on it all. That mysterious butterfly. The watch. (He skipped the part about the insurance card.) Daniela. His *yellow* dream. The pregnancy. The *yellow* balloons. That three of coins. The confirmed pregnancy.

Still, Guillermo did not feel like mentioning the revealing conversation on the third eye with Malva. That would likely have forced him to explain that she was, in fact, his own Reiki coach at a time when he was still reeling from the situation that had just occurred—*Reiki, Jesus, Vilas...*

Remarkably, Guillermo managed to speak uninterrupted—between cheese bites, salami slices, and, every now and then, a few sips from his vermouth glass.

Once both the talk and the appetizers became a thing of the past, Cosme suggested that he consult a doctor. After all, Guillermo might well have been undergoing some stress-related exhaustion as a result of his recent experiences.

"The important thing is—you're alive and kicking, my friend; and you'll continue to be," he added.

Though in unrelated circumstances, he had met similar reactions from other people. He definitely needed to give some serious thought as to that tendency of his to confide his private matters—over and over again—to his *rivals*.

Without another word, they walked to the parking lot. Impetuously, as though he were about to hit a ball during a game, Guillermo asked Cosme:

"Do you happen to remember if you ever went to see *Hair*?"

Cosme left the bag inside the trunk.

"What do you mean by 'seeing hair'?"

"I'm talking about the musical."

"For one second, I thought you were referring to a hair salon—or something of the kind."

Cosme shook the dust off his tired feet, then entered the car. Once inside, he rolled down one of the windows and inquired:

"So, shall we go ahead and sign up for the interclub tournament?"

TEN

A wound to the soul—is that even possible? Does anyone in this world have the ability to either cut through the air or have the wind bow to a harsh word?

Guillermo woke up from his dreams as though he had just emerged from underwater depths. 'Mother, may wise life reenergize you with its vibrancy.' He had dreamed of a mother losing her child—even after her heart had been pierced through with such a ruthless ice pick, her ample breasts were still ready to feed her recently departed baby. What may one say in such circumstances?

He definitely abhorred the thought of that image—along with its suggestive power and the way it had broken through a silence typically associated with dawn—remaining grounded in real life.

What were now the chances of him *undreaming* this? 'Delete' or 'Backspace' choices were either unavailable or insufficient at this time. He might have to make a statement, loud and clear, in his own native language.

Which words—if any at all—could he possibly find to undo something that has already been engraved in the very depths of his universe?

For now, he remained unable to stop thinking about *The Monkey's Paw*—a story by Jacobs that, at some point, Guillermo had resolved to dub *The Monkey's Dough*, considering the Whites' eagerness to prioritize their own welfare above everything else. Besides, Guillermo had been struggling with the idea of a comedian having written such a story in agonizing pain. 'I wish my son could live again,' Ms. White had exclaimed, which had caught a scared Mr. White off guard.

"That's Herbert!" she had screamed. "That's *my* Herbert!" After outrunning his wife to the door, Mr. White had grabbed her arm in an attempt to hold her tightly.

"Where do you think you're going, darling?" he had whispered in a hoarse voice.

"That's my boy—that's *Herbert!*" she had then cried, frantically struggling to escape her husband's firm grasp. "For just one second, I forgot the cemetery is actually two miles down the road. Why are you still holding me? Please let go of my arm! I need to open that door."

"I won't allow you to let *that thing* in," had cried the old man, shaking.

"How dare you be afraid of your own *son*?" she had cried, at the top of her lungs, as she was still struggling. "Let. me. go! I'm coming, my dear Herbert—I'm on my way!"

One of those days, Guillermo actually found himself writing on the steamy mirror in his bathroom: "SHE SHALL BE BACK."

'Will she *truly* be back'? If so, how? In what condition?' He tried hard to erase a sentence that no future steamy shower would likely manage to hide. As a matter of fact, there is no way to *unsend* an email after it has started to make its way out of the outbox folder. Or is there?

'Being back,' 'returning.' Fine—still, *how? In what condition?*

In one of his multiple flashbacks, Guillermo had an emotional encounter with Iris:

"This recipe tastes just like you."

"Uh-hum."

"The framing in that picture reminds me of your eyes."

"Mmh-mm…"

"That delicate fragrance keeps following you everywhere you go."

"Oh. Do you *really* mean it?"

"You and I, together we're so good at making memories."

"Oh, we probably are."

ELEVEN

Using his *Hair* ticket as a bookmark, Guillermo started to 'knock' on his current page of *The Weight of a Butterfly*.

Right now, he was not exactly in the mood to delve into the story. However, the previous lines read:

'He and his sister were orphans. Without their herds nearby, antelopes tend to learn by themselves. He had grown bigger than his male counterparts. / On a wintry, cloudy day, his sister had been apprehended by a daring eagle. She had noticed the bird flying over them around a southern meadow, where some yellowish grass leftovers were still struggling to live on. The sister had been able to spot the eagle despite the overcast sky—something that would have made it next to impossible for her to pinpoint the bird's shade on the ground. Hopeless at this point, the sister had run towards the eagle and had eventually become captured within its tight grip.'

'Pure intuition—that's what it is,' Guillermo reasoned out loud. She was well aware that the bird would go after the one that appeared to be the strongest.

A young palm tree was bending towards the only portion of sky not shaded by the backyard wall.

Guillermo left his book on the grass and headed for the shed. He returned holding a stake in his hands.

'Plus love, too,' he added to his own thoughts. The author, De Luca, had not specified—or, at the very least, Guillermo did not seem to have a recollection—whether the girl was younger or older than her sibling.

Guillermo was now prone to believe that, after witnessing such an act of altruism, the eagle had decided to put an end to its hunting altogether. That it had stopped feeding on helpless preys—a habit which, after all, was in the bird's nature. The eagle seemed to possess many of the attributes that wolf-like human beings lacked. *Homo homini lupus.* 'Man is a wolf to his fellow man.'

It was now Guillermo's second reading of the book. He never knew—in fact, he still does not—what caused him to keep finding the sister's sacrifice so touching.

He placed the stake in such a way that the young palm tree could remain duly braced—and grateful. A remarkable fact about wood is that it can be associated with either life or death. *Homo homini lupus.* A stake can brace a tree. Gallows, conversely, feed on men's lives.

Guillermo entered home, walked towards the library, and placed his *The Weight of the Butterfly* volume among other books by the same author.

Osmosis. It was just then that he noticed the keyword for the first time—*butterfly*.

He woke up from his afternoon nap, still reeling from the vivid images. In one of his dreams, his hand had been bitten by a dog, whereas his palm had been pierced by the animal's fangs. To his surprise, it was not bleeding.

He turned on the computer in an attempt to make sense of his dream: "If the dream involves a dog biting your *right* hand, it generally means that someone close is about to hurt you badly. Such sort of harm tends to be associated with individuals who pretend to be close to you whereas their real purpose is to hurt you. If, conversely, you dream of a dog biting your *left* hand, it may imply that someone close—potentially, an individual pretending to be friends with you—is psychologically harming a person in their circle, compromising qualities traditionally associated with the feminine side of personality, like generosity or trust."

Still, Guillermo was unable to remember which of his hands it was that the dog had bitten in his dream.

He could not stop thinking about Iris. Although that did most definitely not do him any good—as his own children had warned—he resolved to put pen to paper and wrote: *Himalayas*.

That night, Guillermo stayed up until late as he examined multiple pictures of stone-cold landscapes.

Those were the same old sceneries that Iris, like a bolt out of the blue, had brought up in the middle of their memorable family dinner.

The doctor, who apparently doubled as a poet, had said:

"Iris has started to fade in a salty desert—the kind that burns memories away and stitches up the years ahead."

TWELVE

"Dad," Diana said. "In your very own words, your speech might just be branded as *ordinary*."

Guillermo took a bottle of Chardonnay out of the ice bucket, wiped the bottom dry, then poured three glasses of the crisp drink.

Using his tongue, Marco was diligently attempting to spot a bone from the silverside that had become concealed between his teeth. It did not take long before he was successful in his quest.

"What do you mean by *ordinary*?" he asked.

Just in case, he decided to swallow a couple of cleansing breadcrumbs.

For the past few months, they had religiously gathered for luncheon every Sunday. Taking advantage of the spring weather, they decided to ride their bikes to the fishing club.

For a while, the server thoroughly scanned the only empty space on the table. It was just a tiny spot, one onto which it would be somewhat challenging to fit a tray of fries. Using the sleeve of his own jacket for leverage, he managed to slightly move the breadbasket. Guillermo did not appear to even notice.

He stared into space, not being aware of the empty space on the table.

"Birds don't like to look ahead."

That afternoon found them sitting on top of a sandy dune.

"Then, how do they even manage to fly forward?"

"Who knows... By the way, I think I should write a few lines about a beautiful woman that eventually gets lost in a white sea of snow."

Our eyes tend to cry out the salty emptiness of the sea.

"Still, how do they manage not to lose their way?"

Young as they were, they seemed to be pouring all their vital hopes into chords by famous Argentinian band Vox Dei.

Oh, Iris—the very light of my eyes...

"Dad," Diana decided to push forward. "By no means am I implying that you should go around like Elias, riding a cart and a fire horse; still..."

She passed the salad bowl, which contained arugula and Parmesan cheese, among other delicacies.

"I think it should probably be a little more..."

"A salad like this becomes even more delicious when the cheese is finely sliced," Guillermo reflected, as though he was not listening.

"Well, I don't know," Diana carried on. "Maybe a little more..."

"Magical?"

"Yeah—I guess you could just put it that way."

They were sitting next to a window. It was almost seventy degrees—a perfect temperature to leave the window ajar and let the spring flow in.

"I feel like it's lacking that little *something* that your other pieces have. To me, it sounds a bit vague to simply state that 'she shall appear...'"

"And yet, she'll eventually appear."

At that time, the server came out of nowhere to check on the guests, asking whether everything was to their liking.

"I wish I'd been paying closer attention to my dreams," Guillermo admitted. "Or, for that matter, to my creative activity as a writer."

Even after they had confirmed that everything was tasting just fine, the server lingered next to the diners for a few seconds.

"Would that be related to *confirming*, *creating*, or *anticipating* reality?" Marco began to inquire.

Guillermo and Diana started to pay close attention to him, as they eagerly awaited his next words.

"Sir—could we please get a few lemon wedges over here?"

The waiter nodded, finally giving them some much needed privacy.

"I know a woman." Marco said. "She used to write poems that not even she was able to fully understand."

Rising above the blue-and-silvery sea, a gull emerged carrying a crab in its beak.

"I'd assume that those poems you mentioned had probably little to do with her own life."

A number of tourists were rushing for a quick dip in the sea. It might have well been their last day of vacation. 'Sucking the marrow out of life,' as Mr. Keating would put it himself in *Dead Poets Society*, 'doesn't mean choking on the bone.'

"Eventually, the woman put her poems aside— likely in an attempt to let them sit for a while. Later, she learned that she was adopted."

The waiter stopped by briefly to serve the lemon slices.

"So, let me insist—would that be related to *confirming*, *creating*, or *anticipating* reality?"

As Guillermo signed the merchant's copy of the receipt, the server took a quick look around the bar. Then, he bent over slightly and timidly asked:

"Sir, I hope you don't mind my asking, but... are you Mr. Guillermo?"

Partly hidden between his palm and his thumb, the waiter was holding on to what appeared to be a tiny piece of paper folded in two.

Guillermo diligently returned the signed copy of the receipt as he awaited, with an open hand, what he presumed was the consumer's copy. However, he was not *exactly* right. As he stood there in hesitation, the server continued to hold on to the mysterious piece of paper.

"Sir—Ms. Daniela mentioned that you might be in a position to help us."

Eventually, the waiter handed over the note, making it slip through his fingers as someone might probably wait for a carrier pigeon to bring an olive in its beak on its way back.

In bewilderment, Guillermo unfolded the paper carefully. On it, he found a handwritten name, a date of birth, and a mailing address.

"Those are my grandson's contact details," the server explained.

After a silence so thick that no one could possibly have attempted to break, the waiter frantically turned to his table-bussing duties.

What if Ms. Krentz had actually never gotten to write *A Coral Kiss*? Leticia and Manuel had been acquaintances since they were little children. She, a Mar del Plata[3] native, was from Montserrat, whereas he was originally from Balvanera.[4] They had attended elementary, middle, and high school together. It was also in each other's company that they had graduated from the college where they had majored in Ocean Sciences. At the end of their senior year, both friends had resolved to embark on a venturesome expedition (a *prophetic* one, perhaps?) through Southeastern Asia.

The trip seemed to have unearthed what both Leticia and Manuel had apparently been unable to realize until then—that is, how dearly they had secretly been loving each other all along. It was next to ironical that such blatant feelings had gone unnoticed for a long time. 'With a bird-like look.' As they had been trapped—and somewhat blinded—by a map on which they would base their daily adventures, they likely came to believe that this was the way a friendship was meant to be. Growing up with that

3 Mar del Plata is a coastal town located in the province of Buenos Aires, Argentina

4 Montserrat and Balvanera are both neighborhoods of the city of Buenos Aires.

cozy feeling, they never suspected it to be real love. This all came to an end once they had decided to stop their constant rush towards their goals and started to realize the extent of their feelings—and, also, that of their own skins.

The icing on the cake was represented by the "it was just so obvious," "of course," and "at last!" remarks that their teammates would eventually make. The couple wired a message to their respective families in Buenos Aires and finally decided to tie the knot—for life. They would get married in high seas. With multiple travel days being left at that point, the couple was able to enjoy plenty of time for bachelor and bachelorette parties, aside from bombastic celebrations at every restaurant and themed lounge available on the cruise. At some point, all passengers ended up embracing a synesthetic rainbow, which—along with a lively sailing pace—seemed to pump out that kind of ecstatic vibrations in which everyone likes to partake.

THIRTEEN

Walking their bikes, the friends began to head up the boulevard.

"The way I see it," Marco said, "*A Coral Kiss* might be regarded as an anticipatory text."

Either because he was fitter than his children or in a hurry, Guillermo kept walking a few feet ahead of them.

"The reason why you wrote that novel may just be that you were trying to warn us of something unexpected."

"I wouldn't be so sure about that..."

"I guess we just figured that out too late," Diana said.

At that point in their conversation, they noticed that the old greyhound—the one that used to sleep at the club—was following them closely.

"Some would probably argue that it is art that creates reality—*not* the other way around."

"That might just be the case," Marco contributed. "Still, supposing you're an anticipatory writer, wouldn't you be to blame for...?"

"Expertise," Diana interrupted, "is like a hairbrush that life gives you once you've gone terminally bald."

At that point, some guy on a mountain bike rode past them.

"Hey there, Cosme!"

Cosme turned his head, then rode back to their position. After dismounting, he stood next to Guillermo.

"Hey! I was actually about to call you."

Cosme shifted gears on his bike.

"Is everything alright?"

"Well—I guess you could put it that way," Guillermo responded.

"By the way, I *just* signed up for the interclub with that guy from Venezuela."

The clock on the town hall façade showed three o'clock in the afternoon.

"Geez…! Simply stabbing me in the back would've been more than enough—don't you think?"

Cosme pedaled on. However, when he realized that he was leaving Guillermo behind, he began to backtrack.

"I'm really sorry, *Guille*. That kiddo had no one other than myself to go with…"

In all fairness, the Venezuelan guy was in fact a 45-year-old *kiddo*. He had first reached the club on board his own boat.

He was left-handed, as well as a seasoned tennis player. At every shot, his ball would appear to have been propelled by a typhoon. He would mostly play singles. Now, Cosme had apparently decided to break the news barely a week before the tournament. "I'm trying to cool off a bit," Cosme said, then changed gears on his bike and swiftly rode away.

"Are you sure everything's okay, Dad?"

In sporting terms, the situation was dire. Guillermo could still recall the matches they used to play together back in the good old days. In Guillermo's view, Cosme's recent resolution was proof enough of his determination to keep their rivalry alive and kicking.

"I'm yet to find myself a partner for the doubles."

Guillermo had certainly not forgotten those competitions. All along, he had known for a fact that the odds were constantly on Cosme's side—even if that might have held true for only one game, the point is he was still a *winner*.

The boulevard no longer seemed to feature the slope on top of which it used to sit originally. In the distance, the orange-colored tennis court could be glimpsed, surrounded by dozens of eucalypti. Passers-by were also able to hear a number of deafened shots, which tended to be the result of either deflating balls or loosening strings on a player's racket. They all jumped on top of their bike seats.

The greyhound now appeared to have gained the upper hand, serving as an actual seeing-eye dog as he showed the riders the way ahead.

"Look at the dog!" Guillermo said, as though he was having an epiphany.

Guillermo's children gave him a sleepy look, as nap time was approaching.

"Which leads me to think of Cosme's betrayal—that guy's such a hand-biting dog!"

Diana temporarily interrupted his father's reflections, asking Marco whether he had remembered to purchase the morning paper.

"Sure I did."

"Would you mind if I borrowed the magazine for a while?"

"Of course—here you go!"

"I'm *gonna* thrash that fucker!" Guillermo exclaimed.

After Guillermo had made such a blunt statement, neither of them dared to utter a sound until they reached their destination—surrendered as they were to the therapeutic scent of eucalypti.

II

L eticia had her very own opinion about life and death. Her thoughts on this topic, however, could be compared to those of a post or a child who is still learning how to read and write.

"By any chance, do you know what the word *apoptosis* means?" she had once asked Manuel.

"You mean *apotheosis*?"

"No, man—*a-pop-to-sis*."

Leticia provided what she believed was a comprehensive explanation. Since the day we are born, we technically begin to die (yes—*die, die, die!*). That is exactly what the concept of *apoptosis* is about, as it brings to the spotlight the selflessness of cells, which are constantly dying so they can be replaced by younger ones. We are always living and dying— *living* and dying, living and *dying*... Still, we have not quite managed to figure out the place that death should occupy in our lives. May that mean that we are actually *afraid* of life?

"Manuel—would you say that you're afraid of life?"

That *laissez faire, laissez passer* attitude had likely assisted Leticia in becoming a witty woman. She had come to appreciate —and master— the art of improvisation. At one of the on-board shows, she had performed next to a Uruguayan folk singer. Her ample grasp of musical theory allowed for some plucking on her end after the singer had lent her one of his guitars. Beyond that, Leticia also used to be encouraged to impress her audience. She turned out to be such an entertaining and amusing personality that they had no choice but to offer encore performances at the Savannah Hall on the following evenings. 'It has been a long time,' said the captain, 'since I last enjoyed myself on a voyage that much.' Such excitement had eventually turned into widespread joy, infecting every passenger on board.

Leticia and Manuel soon became an inspiration to youngsters. The couple could not help but wonder how that was even possible. For the time being, they had started to dive into uncharted territory, out on the high seas. A watery area all to themselves, one that was yet to be explored—and, also, one that would fill them with unbridled delight.

FOURTEEN

Guillermo's children kept him company as they all walked all the way up to his house. 'Bye, Dad.' 'Take care, guys.' It was time for a nap. Some children were playing cheerfully on the few coastal shores which still remained open to the public.

"See those kids playing over there?" Marco seemed to be thinking out loud. "Along with the land, they could be designated as an actual nature preserve."

Diana smiled.

"Right—at least for the time being..."

"If I were the mayor, I'd take action to prevent excessive development in such a beautiful area."

Eventually, they reached Marco's house. A dog was lying under the shade of a pine tree. He gave them a quick look, then wagged his tail.

"By the way... Don't you think you're being a little too tough on your mother?"

"Who the heck are you talking about?"

"I'm talking about yourself and *your* mother."

"Isn't she *our* mother anymore?"

"Lately, you've been whining a bit too much about everything."

"Okay, you might be right about that. But, what about *her*? It was *her* that decided to leave us behind."

"Well—I'm not sure *decided* would be an accurate word choice here..."

"Okay, then. Let's put it another way—she *prioritized* leaving. Would that sound more accurate to you? She put herself first—that's out of the question."

The dog stood on all fours, then lay down on the opposite side of his body as he turned his head towards the east.

"There's still something else I'd like to mention."

Marco then approached Guillermo's own perception of the cosmos and his alignment with it. At that point, he had started to doubt those predictions, and he was even less convinced about those being valid guesses. He briefly mentioned the issue with the insurance card, placing particular emphasis on Guillermo's related assertion—'it will eventually show up.'

"Still, it never did."

"That's *precisely* what I meant."

"You actually seemed to imply *something else*."

"The way I see it—the frailty of his own life compares to that of a house of cards."

"And now, his mind is apparently set on beating Cosme—he doesn't even have a potential partner in sight, for goodness' sake!"

Diana tied her hair up high into a bun.

"As for that stuff you mentioned—I honestly don't know what to say, Marco…"

"Trusting him might be the only right-*ish* choice at this point."

"I'll give it some thought, though. Now, I need to run. Take care."

"Wait. Didn't you want to borrow my magazine?"

"Oh, sure. I almost forgot. Thanks, then!"

III

A celebratory atmosphere was widespread among passengers and crew alike. The captain had decided on a last-minute change of course. For a few hours, the ship would remain anchored off a paradise-like island highlighted on the sailing screen. Three boats had been rigged. On those, a selected few—mostly those with an *aloha* state of mind—would be heading for a beach which, so far, appeared to have been spared of visitors' footprints.

A native islander was waiting for their arrival by the shore. Actually, he seemed to have been there all along—it was not long before Guillermo drew a cunning analogy between the indigenous individual and the three monks in Tolstoy's account. The local appeared to own one of those human-powered vehicles. As for the surrounding scenery, it could not have been more idyllic.

Trusting the captain as their improvised officiant, Leticia and Manuel pledged to one another that they would remain loyal to each other 'till death did them part,' as they laughed and daydreamed. The couple raised a toast with some champagne provided by the company, following a call with the operator.

Pictures of the happy event would eventually become publicized on the corporate website. After all, it would seem like the company was truly committed to making travelers' dreams come true.

FIFTEEN

Guillermo eventually managed to make his way into a seemingly forgotten boulevard. At that point, time appeared to have come to a halt. He immediately realized how wrong he was. Rather than stop, time was actually going backwards—approximately, twenty years earlier. Nobody in their right mind would have elected to travel back then.

That day, he decided to skip his restful afternoon nap. After all, the recent issue with Cosme would likely have given him a hard time in attempting to catch some z's. 'Why do I continue to get upset over the most insignificant of things?' Even though he was actively aiming at developing a calmer attitude towards life, he would constantly have to face comparable situations, which would typically catch him off guard and immediately take away his inner peace.

At the end of the day, however, what were upsetting situations compared to Iris' absence? Unsuccessful in his quest for a potential explanation, he had eventually come to terms with life being similar to a pendulum, incessantly meandering along deep and shallow matters.

Under his arm, Guillermo was carrying his copy of Czeslaw Milosz's book. At some point, he had resolved to transfer his *Hair*-ticket bookmark from *The Weight of the Butterfly* into *The Issa Valley*. 'Now, once my poetry is back around in Poland, it won't feel right unless I admit how much I owe to solitude. As hard as it may be to accept at first, it can definitely become rewarding in the long run. It is also my belief that written words are meaningless unless one fully embraces bitterness, said solitude, and loss,' Milosz reflected in his preface to the book.

Oh, that good old *Hair* ticket, and that bewitching pink quartz pebble... Lately, he had been enjoying keeping those within reach at all times.

As he walked on following the neglected boulevard, the shades of green started to become increasingly darker. Deep into the lush scenery, Guillermo finally began to cool down.

"Guillermo—were you aware...?"

"Of what?"

"That the colors in playdough become brown once they've all been mixed up."

"Uh-huh."

"Same as in hummus, right?"

"Yeah—that's one way to put it."

"'You are dust, and unto dust you shall return.'"

"So true..."

A slender stream of fresh water had somehow made it to the riverbed. The sloping terrain provided the tiny creek with a strength similar to that of its Amazonian counterparts.

Guillermo took a seat on a fallen trunk. Below, the thin, yet powerful stream kept flowing. He left his book on the snow-white sand. Then, he attempted to plunge one of his hands into the cool water—firstly two fingers, then five, finally the whole palm. He raised his pink quartz pebble towards the only ray of sunshine that had managed to pierce through the powerful surrounding lushness.

He sat up, planting his foot firmly against a smooth rock covered by a thin layer of moss—and, eventually, he stumbled. Resembling a bird, he opened his arms wide in an attempt to keep flying. Keeping pace with its owner's movements, the book opened as swiftly as the Argentinian and Uruguayan large accordion known as *bandoneón*.

At the intersection of three potential pathways, Guillermo eventually opted for the road less traveled. At that point, the voice of the sea became nothing but a distant roar. He could easily recognize the constant hooting of one of the owls in the bell tower. The lovely crispness of freshly cut grass welcomed him. *Apoptosis*—here it was! A green creation which in turn featured the selflessness present in life and death. Then, he fleetingly thought of Leticia—one of the literary characters that he had created himself—

who had chosen to pursue a degree in Ocean Sciences, a discipline intrinsically associated with *creation*.

'I have no control whatsoever over the beat of my soul.' That sentence now seemed to be more appropriate than ever. Malva had assured him that his ascended master would be staying by his side every time he wrote. For the time being, Guillermo had become lost amidst a sea of tangled green shades. What could that mean, aside from providing some reliable evidence regarding Leticia's own experiences? At that moment, he felt an irrepressible urge to pray. He was able to locate a cave, which he decided to use as his own makeshift sanctuary. After kneeling down and praying in an unprecedented manner, he could not help but weep uncontrollably until grief met its own dusk.

Primitive forces of nature remained a mystery to Guillermo. At the end of the day, that bountiful promenade became an accurate allegory of himself.

Upon return to urban life, Guillermo realized that the *Hair* ticket was nowhere to be found between the book's pages. He paused for a short while, clearly hurt by the loss. He really wanted to retrace his steps, but it was already too late.

IV

Between kisses and necklaces designed out of paper flowers. As the model citizen from Mar de Plata she was, Leticia got on her rickshaw and, from up there, started to recite a poem by Alfonsina Storni:

'Deep down on the seabed,
One can find a house of glass.
One that overlooks
A promenade
Of madrepores.
At five sharp,
A big golden fish
Likes to stop by and greet me.

He also hands me
A red bouquet
Of coral flowers.

I sleep in a bed
Slightly bluer
Than the sea.
Through the glass,
An octopus

Likes to wink at me. In the green woods
Surrounding me
—Ding, dong… ding, ding—
Mother-of-pearl mermaids
As green as the sea
Like to swing and sing.And, all over my head,
The spiky peaks of the sea
Like to burn at dusk.'

Then, inebriated with both joy and champagne, she ran towards the deep sea. To no avail, the driver of the vehicle did everything he possibly could—in his own manners and language—to warn against her impulse.

A dead coral cut one of her feet open—from its very heel all the way up to the crossroad of its toes.

SIXTEEN

Diana found her Dad comfortably sitting on a recliner by the swimming pool. The bottom-cleaning equipment was still sitting on the deck.

"Dad."

Birds were tweeting incessantly that day. It would appear that spring was making them hectic. They would fly from a magnolia to an olive branch, then to a jacaranda tree—and so on and so forth.

"My baby girl—I didn't hear you coming."

It did not take too long before Diana perceived the unique soundtrack for the day.

"Your feathery friends seem excited, huh?"

"It seems they are, indeed!" Guillermo said, unable to conceal a genuine smile.

By then, it had become apparent to Diana that her father was not being himself. He was holding a letter that dangled from his fingers. Guillermo's grip of the envelope affected the pose of his hand, his arm, and even his shoulder.

"Dad," Diana said, "you really should go for a tiebreaker."

"What do you mean by that?

"Just go for a tiebreaker—an unbalance, a tipping of the scales."

"So, what was your final score with Marco?"

"One-one—just what everyone would expect at this point."

"Great. We should score some penalties, then."

"Dad, please stop messing around, will you?"

"What do you want me to do?"

"Just vote—go ahead and make the right decision."

"Alrighty. So, what right decision am I supposed to make *right now*?"

"Where are you *gonna* spend your Christmas holidays?"

"Christmas?"

"Exactly—that's what I just said."

"It's barely November, for goodness' sake!"

"You know me. I like to plan for everything well in advance."

"What does it matter?"

"I just wanted to know at whose place you'd like to spend the holidays..."

"While you did ask me that, you still forgot to mention what my options are."

"Well. We may either stay here or go to a restaurant."

"What about yourself? Which plan do you like best?"

"To be honest, I don't think I'd really enjoy spending this time of year at home."

The slippery letter (*The Monkey's Paw... Mrs. White*) caused Guillermo to swiftly change the pose of his fingers, hand, arm, and shoulder.

"Dad. What's *that*?"

"Oh. *This*?" he exclaimed as he handed the papery keepsake to Diana. "This is actually for you."

Diana looked at the front of the envelope, eventually focusing on the familiar handwriting. She took a look at the back, then another look at the front. As she was examining the back of the envelope and reexamining its front, her gaze met that of his father. Guillermo's eyes appeared focused and seemed to mirror his daughter's every move; however, they were neither present on the spot nor anywhere else.

V

The boat was far from equipped with the necessary tools that would have allowed the sailors to face the razor-sharp coral reefs. After some deliberation, they decided to carry Leticia aboard the vehicle and drive her to the nearest hospital, which was a full four miles away. Away was also the right word to define the cruise that had set sail in hopes of picking them up at the next anchoring stop.

The second part of the novel focused on the twists and turns of the bizarre pilgrimage of both the driver, Manuel, and Leticia—who left behind marks of lipstick on the wild sand.

Guillermo had decided to incorporate that turn of events into his own plot—a story of coral, after attending a family constellation. The family regarded as an actual constellation. Back then, they had talked about those relatives that were no longer among the living—a little bit of everything, actually. The deceased relative that has already reached the heights of heaven is one that—as the constellator would say—struggles to drag the living into their own reality. This can be due to rooted melancholy, or the fact that he yearns for being remembered in the life of the living. Said relative certainly acts like this for the sake of love; however, this may be regarded as a *misdirected* kind of love. Relatedly, they recalled the story of some individual that, not having been valued by his own family, ultimately fell into oblivion after he passed away. That person, bearing a pain comparable to that of an exile, seemed to enjoy luring the living to himself. The constellator had said that all they needed to do was to keep the memory of the decease alive—in other words, warmly remember him—so that he would not attract the living to the life (wait—*life*!?) of the dead.

Guillermo used to fantasize about the idea of the dead coral attempting to draw Leticia to itself. The *reason* was bound to be revealed in the third part of the novel.

SEVENTEEN

Diana mentioned that she would read the letter later. Guillermo was tempted to ask her to open it—right there and then. He could not fight the feeling that the envelope was a carrier of bad news. He also remained willing to support her in case the letter might involve misfortune.

Numerous graffiti could be seen crawling up the walls of the Normal School:

*'In this city, people seem to bear suicide better
than they face mental ailments.'*

"That pigeon," Iris said, "just came back carrying an olive branch on its beak."

"That actually means *life*," Guillermo exclaimed. "That is synonymous with life."

"The branch was bare, though."

'In this city, my child, most people seem unable to bear the blues—still, they tend to do better when faced by the murky pits of suicide—the radical nature of suicide. Apparently, they believe that being dead is actually preferable to limping or being blind in one eye, insane, poor, old, an autistic, or even a homosexual.'

"She's not coming back, Dad. She is no longer the person you used to know."

"What do you mean, Diana? How wouldn't she have stayed the same...?"

All of a sudden, as Diana finally resolved to read the letter, *now* became *then*. It was a Himalayan-style postcard that had been sent from the city of Kathmandu, in Nepal.

'I love you, my beloved daughter.'

The postscript read:

'Here, mental illness is regarded as an emergency of the soul.'

The words in the postcard were sufficient to put Diana's heart at peace. Until then, she had not had much opportunity for second thoughts. She had never fully internalized the fact that her mother had spent her last days in utter despair. However, she could now realize how her mother's hope had actually drifted into the darkness of the ocean a long time ago.

At that point, Diana had nothing but a single project in mind—waiting. She spent the rest of her day smelling the flowers—enjoying a sense of calm that radiated all the way down and into her chest. As dinner time approached, Diana entertained the fleeting thought of calling her father and her brother to update them on her thoughts. Eventually, however, she resolved to refrain from doing so—after all, they had most likely received their own postcards by then.

EIGHTEEN

Guillermo woke up, already deep in his thoughts. He found himself thinking about cassava—the actual word *cassava*. Months earlier, he had a similar experience, this time related to *adzuki beans*. All of a sudden, everything in his life had started to revolve around *adzuki beans* for him. No matter how fleeting, his obsession eventually lasted for a week or two.

Hi there, adzuki beans.

During such a memorable week—needless to say—Guillermo would not go around greeting and addressing every passer-by in that fashion. Apparently, the unconventional phrase solely applied to a number of children—and also, to be precise, adults who looked like children to him and a number of animals—pets, for the most part.

The storekeeper kept his demeanor as rough as sandpaper. Finely chopped, no ice.

That was probably nothing to write home about, though.

"How's things going today, *Mr. Borges*?"

He seemed to enjoy feeding his own ego on tiny verbal mischiefs. As it appeared, those likely assisted him in keeping body and soul together through the end of his shift.

"I visited Mar del Plata yesterday," he said. "I checked out a new bookstore, and made sure to ask about your latest book..."

"Interesting. Yesterday, though, I didn't happen to be in the area."

In a gentle voice, not fully comfortable with the idea of abruptly switching gears, Guillermo gathered his courage and ordered: "Can I please get half a pound of mortadella?"

"Sure thing. Still, I was asking about your books."

"I'm afraid those books you mention are nowhere to be seen."

"Alrighty, then. Half a pound, you said, right? I'll be right back... See, honey?—my buddy here is a celebrity. I told you!"

Oblivious to the storekeeper's words, Guillermo attempted to locate one of his favorite cassava baskets—already anticipating its deliciousness after finely slicing, then pan-frying the vegetable.

The merchant's wife entered the store from the back door. She was carrying a platter full of fried schnitzel.

"Good morning, everyone!"

"Good morning."

She carefully placed the platter inside the display refrigerator.

"Are you next in line?"

"Don't worry, babe—I got this."

"You do look busy slicing that meat, though. How can I help you today, sir?"

"I'm trying to find some cassava."

"You'll find that outdoors, right by the entrance," the woman said. "Wait a sec—I'll get a knife to check on the quality of the produce."

They both headed outside.

Guillermo could feel the salty breeze caressing his forehead.

"Are you planning on publishing any books in the future? I got all of your books so far!"

"Really? I had no idea you liked reading."

"I *love* it!"

"Well… To be honest, I still haven't made any plans in terms of future publications…"

"*Come on, Guillermo, cut it out. You're running behind schedule!*" he thought to himself.

"Do you have any recommendations for us to read?" the storekeeper's husband jumped in.

"*The price list would be a great read to start with, don't you think!?*" Guillermo thought—almost out loud—for the second time in a row.

"You saw that? My hubby here has a good ear, doesn't he?" the lady exclaimed. "I wish he would put that gift of his to good use, though…" she said as she scraped a cassava root with her knife. "See? This one here looks top quality—the peel easily comes off."

They walked back into the store. The storekeeper was holding an imposing cleaver. He kept transferring the tool clumsily from one of his hands to the other. He then started to work on a piece of creamy cheese.

"So, how's Iris been doing?" the merchant asked.

His wife looked at him, feeling sorry for her very own husband. She could not help feeling compassion for him sometimes.

"I was just telling her the other day," he pointed at his wife with the edge of the cleaver. "It takes a brave man to go looking for her.

Somewhat disgruntled, the lady responded: 'I disagree—a brave man is the one that once let her go and will patiently wait for her to come back.' Whose side are you on, sir?"

"I'd personally side with the idea that— cassava is best fried in garlic-flavored oil."

"Well put, sir," the storekeeper's wife said, then added. "If you don't hurry up, that cheese is *gonna* melt."

"Is there anything else I can do for you?"

"I'd like some salami, please."

"By the way—did I mention Cosme came here yesterday?" the storekeeper recalled.

Guillermo noticed that the merchant had the shape of the counter imprinted on his shirt. He had never seen the man doing anything other than moving back and forth around that store.

"He mentioned you guys might just be the next winners at the tournament."

"Well, that remains to be seen. First, we'll need to play," Guillermo said.

"... And I told him, 'Well, I'm happy for both you and Guillermo.' That's when he went ahead and told me."

Guillermo tried to stick with his professional demeanor.

"I'll also get some garlic."

The woman provided him with a garlic bulb from the string.

"I actually tried to play once, myself..." the storekeeper started to recall as his wife rushed to ask the customer, once again, whether he was searching for anything else.

"No, thanks. I think that's pretty much all I need for now."

Guillermo's attention was drawn by a picture of a yogurt commercial that was taped to the store wall: 'If you feel like it, think no more and go for it!'

That was a *yogurt* commercial! The last time he had seen such a message on a commercial, that had been to advertise some brand of beer.

At this point, Guillermo was aware that the storekeeper would probably never stop overwhelming him with questions. However, he was just too preoccupied dwelling on the *feeling*—not the word itself, but rather its meaning, as well as the actual *feeling* that he would succumb to every time that word played in his head. Guillermo liked to compare this to a palm flower like the ones growing in his lawn: the subtlest touch was enough to send thousands of seeds spreading through the air.

He then found himself paying for the cassava and the garlic bulb and being presented with his change. He was still not paying attention to the storekeeper's words, deep in thought as he was in his obsession with the *feeling*.

At some point in history, the word must have been deprived of its original meaning. Beer commercials might well be to blame—and even certain religions.

Ever since he was a high schooler himself, Guillermo had never forgotten the phrase that one of his teachers had once mentioned:

"You can't just live doing what you *feel* like."

He then recalled his old mentor as he stepped back to take a closer look at him.

"Rather the opposite, sir" Guillermo had argued. "I've grown increasingly convinced that it's actually in everyone's best interest to let our feelings do the talk."

And, right now, Guillermo's feelings were urging him to ask the storekeeper to leave him alone.

NINETEEN

"**I**s there anything wrong?"

"I don't know."

"Why are you crying?"

"I'd rather not tell you."

She observed the three fishermen on the horizon. They appeared to have been nailed to planks made of air and seawater.

"There's something I saw that is just too hard to talk about."

"What's that?"

"I'm not ready to tell you, yet."

"How about tomorrow?"

"No promises. Tell me something good, please—I could really use some niceties at the moment."

He held her hand in those navy-blue depths. He thought of his teenage years. He also thought of Juan Salvador Gaviota.

"Yesterday," he mentioned, "a kid approached me on the street and told me he had designed some sort of GPS to track people's souls."

Iris regrouped as she started to collect her fishing network, which looked both plentiful and miraculous.

"That's something nice, indeed... So, everything should be okay—soon."

TWENTY

Guillermo kept on walking, surrounded as he was by the echo of the recent chit-chatting back at the store. With barely a handful of days left, he was yet to find himself a partner for the tennis doubles. Of his high school former classmates, none seemed to be into 'traditional' tennis these days. One of them was a pelota player, while another one had a penchant for paddle tennis.

As a likely result of his rather classical background, Guillermo had a gut feeling that he should choose the former as a partner. His intuition kept telling him that, should he eventually decide on the *pelotari*, the Atlantic would eventually become the resting place of dozens of successful balls.

He walked past the block, using his cassava basket as a racket to practice his best forehand and backhand strokes. As he approached the next block, he was suddenly attacked by a fierce dog. In an attempt to avoid greater evils, he resolved to wrap the cassava basket with a plastic bag, along with the garlic bulb.

Guillermo continued to walk in close proximity to the buildings, which turned out to be a valuable source of bountiful shade. At that point, he could not help feeling a sense of distraction, the uncertainties regarding the letter from Iris still haunting his mind.

He decided to stop and take a deep breath. It felt like he was grasping at the last straws of courage that kept holding him together. He crouched down next to the wall, letting the sun dry the tears behind his dark glasses.

All this time, he had pretended to be more absent-minded than he actually was. He remained unable to shake the feeling that bad tidings were on their way. Also, everything seemed to indicate that, this time around, Diana would not be the bearer of unwelcome news.

Could all of Guillermo's suffering be due to insufficient love? Might this eventually result in him growing his own love for others? Had he been acting in a merciless, prejudiced manner against his loved ones? Even though he was now far from being a champion, Guillermo knew that he would get there someday.

At this point, forgiving Cosme remained the right thing to do. Guillermo had reached such a conclusion after perusing his copy of A Course in Miracles:

Do not exclude anyone from your love. If you did, you would be unwelcoming to the Holy Ghost somewhere in your mind. You would be excluding yourself from His healing power. If you do not offer your love in its entirety, you will never attain full healing.

Needless to say, Guillermo also needed to forgive the storekeeper. He had to thank him for the constant scorning on his own end. He was grateful for the opportunity to keep sanding off the many spikes in his heart.

He had to forgive, indeed—and yet, that was a challenging process. Resembling one of the characters from his recent readings, Guillermo had been raised within a strict "Western Christian" framework. And now, those rock-solid foundations—in which happiness seemed to have no place—were starting to collapse as a result of the rust left behind by whatever he used to love.

As though his life were a nest of ovenbirds, he needed to build new foundations on perishable materials like adobe and straw, more in tune with his own changing existence.

By the time he arrived home, he had resolved to call her:

"Is that a letter from Iris? Is she saying hi to us?"

VI

Along the four-mile stretch that runs from the beach to the hospital, the moujik observed how Leticia's blood continued to dot the road, as though the vital fluid were actually fertilizing the soil in the form of godsent meanders.

For locals, things tend to be just the way they are. They find no point in resisting the circumstances. Will weak reeds ever be capable of outcompeting strong winds? The universe always seems to know better.

Using his broken English, the moujik attempted to narrate an old legend involving a coral:

'Corals end up dying on the beach, and it is only with the kiss of a beautiful woman that they will have an opportunity to revive. They will patiently await their moment—for seconds, centuries, or even longer. Corals like to kiss passionately using their razor-sharp coating— the only possible action within their reach. The blood of a beautiful woman returns them to life, no matter how deep or shallow that may be. That is how they reincarnate—or resurrect, depending on their creed—in order to pursue a second life.'

In a delusion that featured scorching sands, Leticia rested her hand on the moujik's shoulder as she asked:

"Is this supposed to be for the better?"

"Of course, my lady—it's always been that way."

Pointing with his thumb over his shoulder, the moujik added that, centuries ago, an Anglican man had penned a sentence on the rear board of his cart: *'All shall be well, and all shall be well, and all manner of things shall be well.'*

"See, my lady? That's the way it's always been..."

After listening to such natural and solemn words, the bride eventually surrendered to the somnolence brought about by both her splendid wedding and a body temperature that had started to develop.

TWENTY-ONE

"Could that be regarded as shortsightedness of the soul?"

"Not of the soul proper—our souls were perfectly designed. They just require experiences to feed on."

"So, that would be rather...?"

"Shortsightedness of the heart."

"When I cry, I seem unable to figure out where my tears come from. The thing is—I've known you for quite a while, ever since I was seventeen."

"Yes—it's been a minute, indeed."

"I wonder what's left of those teenagers we used to be..."

"We're still the same—at heart."

"So, what happened to us?"

"I just told you—we're both suffering from shortsightedness of the heart."

TWENTY-TWO

Diana's house sat on a boulevard known as Paseo del Levante. The name of the street—which would roughly translate as 'Easterly Promenade'—might be thought of as a broken string in the symphony of a seven-house microclimate. Neither the Royal Spanish Academy nor the neighbors were successful in dodging the original purpose shown by the name: 'Levante: (Spanish. masculine) 1) Cardinal point from where the sun rises on the equinoxes. Synonyms: East, Orient. 2) Part of a country, territory, or other place that faces said point.'

The street was notably broad, even more so than any of its local counterparts. This allowed neighbors and visitors alike to behold the magnificence of the European-style mansions. Guillermo could not help but be attracted to the house with the blue tiles. Diana's study room overlooked the sea. The hardwood floors came from white oak timber that she had purchased at an antiques store. There was a Wilton rug under the desk where she liked to work on her translations.

Captivated by the coastal landscape, Guillermo was standing in front of the window when Diana briefly entered the room. As she was crossing the threshold, she said:

"I found it hanging over the nightstand."

She was carrying the envelope, the postcard, and a piece of paper—a thin one, one of those that are typically used for tracing purposes.

"It turns out she apparently isn't..." Diana mentioned. "Iris is *not* saying hi to everyone."

Guillermo suddenly ceased his contemplation of the sea. He approached the desk and slightly leaned on it using both the index and middle fingers on his left hand.

"Are you working on a Catalan translation?" he asked, searching for traces of writing on the multiple whiteboards that dotted the walls.

Diana handed him the postcard. He held it as a compassionate relative holding the hands of a loved one that is in pain.

"What a beautiful picture," he said, standing still, as he tried to summon the courage to look at the back of the postcard. "As for these little flags..."

The flags appeared to be trapped in the everlasting snow of the Himalayas.

"Those are known as prayer flags," Diana said.

"I find them extremely captivating."

"Now, if you're ready, go ahead and look at the back."

The postcard appeared to come as the bearer of bad news. Guillermo attempted to catch a glimpse of his daughter's countenance. *IT SHALL COME BACK... IT SHALL COME BACK... The Monkey's Paw.* He left the room but returned immediately, tormented by uncertainty—and, especially, the impending confirmation of his own misfortune, which his fingertips had already started to decipher.

Despite the deep fear, Guillermo was able to validate—once again—the presence of a loving, higher intelligence that appeared to embrace his whole self. Even though he had intended to—*creatively?*—create a painful reality, he still felt like he was being spared, protected by some sort of good-prone cosmic consciousness.

Shaken by his emotions, he said:

"What your mother wrote is really beautiful..."

"It is, indeed—you can get a sense of how happy I am."

"It definitely shows!"

"Actually, *happy* would be an understatement."

Once again, Guillermo checked the front of the postcard, then the back. He made sure to take his time to admire the beloved handwriting.

"It looks like she's not saying hi to anyone in particular..."

"So, didn't you and Marco get your own letters?"

"No—at least, I didn't."

Diana held the tracing paper between her slender fingers. The piece carried a message in the shape of three solid lines. At the bottom, Iris revealed herself in her unique, sweet, unembodied handwriting. There was also a number—or probably a code.

Diana looked straight into her father's eyes:

"How's it going with your statements and stuff?" she asked, handing him the golden-lined message.

Faced with the sacred revelation, Guillermo began to feel the fear seizing him once again.

VII

Leticia felt the salty sands as they continued to penetrate deep into her wound. She wished the sea were made of sugar—or spiderweb...

By the time they arrived at the hospital, Leticia looked completely wrecked by the fever. At the admissions desk, Manuel was politely requested to provide all the necessary documentation, including the patient's passport and insurance details. As it turned out, all such documents had been left behind on board the cruise ship. All Manuel had now left from the voyage was that ludicrous garland of paper flowers, still hanging from his neck.

All that was now left was Leticia's fever—in addition to Guillermo's own confusion.

"She is from Montserrat, whereas I come from Balvanera," he was rumored to be whispering as he wandered around the hallways.

TWENTY-THREE

"You should cherish what you have."

"Then, should I cherish my own emptiness? That feels like tasteless steam emanating all the way up from the depths of my soul. Do you think I really need to cherish that?"

"You now resemble Jack in Shadowlands."

"I'm no longer looking forward to potential experiences."

"There's apparently no way to bridge the gap between theory and practice..."

"Bridges tend to be—lovingly—blown up by a higher power."

"... As for the sky, it likes to fill its lungs with air as it exposes its delicate ribs..."

"Alright—if you say so..."

TWENTY-FOUR

The windchime announced Guillermo's arrival. By the doorstep, there was a mandala made of recycled tiles. He heard Malva's steps approaching. In a rather straightforward manner, she asked what the weather was like outside. Guillermo replied to the best of his skin's ability—it felt pleasantly breezy.

"That's nice. Then, feel free to leave the door open."

A lady passed by on her bicycle, visibly struggling to keep the strong headwinds at bay. Strands of hair stalked the corners of her mouth, eventually taking aim at her eyes. Though thin, tree branches remained firm in their peaceful resistance. The hydrangeas in the central flowerbed looked as still as a painting.

"See? We humans are the only living beings that seem to be disturbed by wind," Guillermo said.

He sat at his desk, as Malva continued to stare at the sea through the open door. Guillermo made himself comfortable in his chair, inadvertently adopting Malva's pose. A few unremarkable seconds went by. Maya leaned her chin against the palm of her hand as she sighed:

"Are you in a hurry?"

"I don't know. You keep asking me the same question!"

At that moment, a child walking by on the sidewalk leaned out to the courtyard, rang the windchime mischievously, and fled the scene. Shaken by such an unanticipated storm, the wooden tubes began to play what sounded like Turkish rhythms.

"Look at that kiddo!"

A new quote had appeared on the wall:

'All shall be well, and all shall be well, and
all manner of things shall be well.'
Julian of Norwich

"What's the meaning of that?"

"It's just a quote."

"I find it relevant to one of my novels," Guillermo said, immediately correcting course. "I used to, anyways."

"But you're not the author, right?"

"No—of course I'm not."

"Then—why did you say, 'I used to, anyways'?"

"What do you mean?"

"I'm talking about the connection between that quote and your novel."

"I just burned it."

Malva raised her eyebrows as though she was missing something. For the duration of the pause, the sea could be heard clearly as it splashed against the boardwalk.

"I just had to give it up."

"When was that?"

"Why don't we talk about this some other time?"

"Okay," Malva said, yet secretly longing for more.

"Can you believe," Guillermo said suddenly, "that Tibetan tapestry actually influenced her decision on the trip?"

Malva bent her head and caressed the Gobelins upholstery, as though she was petting a puppy.

"You mean *this* tapestry?"

"Yes."

"How long since she's been gone?"

"Thirty-one days—no more and no less."

"Bye, ma'am!" the kid yelled, this time not striking the chime. "That kid always likes to do the same thing," Malva explained. "Whenever he comes back, he never rings the chime. But shortly, he'll just come back and bang it again." "Interesting." Guillermo said. He looked down, staring at the bewitching mapping of his own hands.

"What's wrong?"

"What do I know..."

Guillermo picked up the tiny wooden hammer, causing the metal rod to vibrate. The long sound of the *Ti* filled the room. As the sound began to fade— muffled between the many cushions and corners in the room—Malva asked:

"What's become of your third-eye opening, as well as those statements?"

Guillermo fished in his pockets for the note that Iris had written to Diana. Surprisingly, it showed no fold marks. He treated the note just as delicately as if it had been the holy communion.

"Diana believes Iris wants me to travel to Kathmandu."

"So you can pick her up?"

"No. Well, at least she didn't mention that exactly. She keeps saying those numbers make up an actual phone number."

"So?"

IT SHALL COME BACK... IT SHALL COME BACK... IT SHALL COME BACK... IT SHALL COME BACK... IT WILL COME BACK...

At that point, Guillermo was also afraid of something else. He did not even dare to say the word, lest that might make his fears come true.

TWENTY-FIVE

At that point, Guillermo had realized that not everything was entirely true. The wings of his nose felt stiff. Breaking into Iris' freedom did not seem like the right thing to do. After all, she had decided to leave without asking anyone. She should therefore be able to return in her own terms.

"I can't intrude on her freedom."

"Isn't that what pride is all about?"

"I don't know."

He grabbed the piece of tracing paper. The Tibetan tapestry remained clearly visible through it. The numbers on the note seemed to be exact coordinates engraved between the stone, the snow, and the sky. The short journey separating the paper and the tapestry caused him to shiver.

"Do cry as much as you need to."

"I'm not crying, Malva. I'm not sure what this is all about."

After all, that was nothing but a series of figures on a brief note. Should this have been a phone number, Iris would most likely have mentioned that.

"Why do you keep referring to Iris as *she*?"

'Take care of me the same way you would
take care of the apple of your eye;
hide me beneath the shade of your own wings.'

Guillermo swiped his hand under his mouth. His index finger remained placed across his lips. He relaxed his hand as the knot in his stomach began to loosen up.

"What if she's no longer the same Iris I used to know?"

"We're never the same—we die every day, without fail, in order to remain alive."

"That sounds like something you read online, I guess."

"That's not the point, right?"

A dead silence came from the street. Even though the wind had ceased, the sea was no longer audible in the distance.

"It'll be ultimately up to you to figure it out."

Guillermo felt overwhelmed by an ocean of memories. Deep inside, he could sense a rage similar to that of a revolving door. An inch below his belly button, his gut felt like it was getting pierced by the Tibetan ridges. "You'll need to figure this out by yourself," Malva kept saying. "No one will ever give you the answer."

Now, he felt as though he was playing the part of Robert S. Leonard, Neil Perry, in *Dead Poets Society*:

"I'm trapped," the guy said.

Actually, he did not get to *say* anything—he just *moaned*.

He wanted to perform—that was his one true passion. Now, his demeanor seemed to mirror that of Puck, or Robin Goodfellow, from the Shakespearian comedy *A Midsummer Night's Dream*. A comedy, the threshold of drama for Neil Perry. All to himself.

He did want to perform—that was his one true passion, indeed. And yet, his father had other plans for him.

"I'm trapped," the character on stage would moan.

"I'm trapped," Guillermo emulated. He then added, "I'm also scared to death."

TWENTY-SIX

*H*er forehead was dotted with a series of freckles, resembling a crown. She was about to give birth to baby Diana, but her facial expression conveyed the calmness of Maria de Mdugorje.

"Are you afraid?" Guillermo confessed he was. He truly was. Iris smiled as she stroked the back of Guillermo's hand. She gently brought his hand to her face and began to caress it with her lips.

Guillermo put a white cloth over Iris' forehead, ensuring not to cover the starry crown that he liked so much.

"You ever heard about that story of a knife," Iris began to ask, "that got persuaded not to chop onions?"

It was just like Iris to make that sort of witty remarks. She would have unrivaled expertise in lightening the mood.

"A steel knife was advised against chopping onions so it wouldn't end up damaging its powerful blade. The knife had remained mindful of this for most of its life. One day, a seasoned utility peer went, 'Dude—that steel of yours was tempered at almost one thousand degrees. You seriously think the acidity of an onion will hurt you?'"

Aware of the knife's fate, the sweat on Iris' forehead reappeared, resembling twelve tiny stars.

"*Don't be afraid,*" Iris said. "*It's just our daughter that's coming.*"

TWENTY-SEVEN

Once the wind stopped blowing, an Atlantic moisture started to fill the place.

The 'sidewalk globetrotter'—as Guillermo and Malva would eventually dub the mischievous child—reappeared, hit the chime, and ran away. Malva began to chase him.

Guillermo realized Malva's reaction and also headed outdoors.

He saw Malva intermittently holding the child's hand and patting his shoulder. Seeing confusion written all over Guillermo's face, Malva clarified that she just wanted to ask the child a question:

"You *kiddo*—I noticed you seem to like my windchimes. Would you like to have one?"

"No, ma'am. I'm good."

"Alrighty, then. Bye."

"Bye, ma'am."

"You see, Guillermo?"

"What, *ma'am*?"

"Ain't that funny? As it turns out, that kid wasn't interested in getting one of my chimes—he's just a pure adrenalin seeker."

"Right," Guillermo agreed.

"How many days has it been since Iris left?"

"Thirty-one."

"You need to play the lottery," Malva said. "It might just be the right time."

VIII

The nurse wondered out loud how Manuel had managed to carry the patient in his arms for a four-mile stretch. He talked about the moujik and the vehicle. The woman pointed out that, in such situations, individuals seem to turn their weakness into strength. Manuel mentioned that the moujik's vehicle had a reassuring message engraved saying that everything would be fine. "All the better," said the nurse.

Manuel lay back on a wooden bench in the hallway. He immediately fell asleep, but he did not rest. The Tolstoyan monk kept pointing his finger at the seabed. The joy of celebrating life, the wedding, hindered Manuel from observing an essential warning—the kiss of coral, an actual celebration of death.

He woke up promptly. In barely a five-minute lapse, he contemplated both life and death. He sat, resting his back and his neck against the wall. He entered one of those feverish states that no thermometer could ever detect.

"I'm gripped by unspeakable fear," he told Leticia this time. "I feel like a top spinning in the air, wondering where it'll end up."

"Why are you talking in terms of *ending up*? Wouldn't the term *landing* be more appropriate?"

"You've got a point. Still—what if the outcome involves losing it all?

Manuel, my love—such an inscription is nowhere to be seen on the spinning top.

Following that remark, Leticia equipped herself with a probe, a Foley catheter, and a cannula. Before covering her mouth with the respirator, she whispered, "Such an inscription is nowhere to be seen in real life."

TWENTY-EIGHT

Guillermo found himself thinking of the number thirty-one. What if that was actually a message for him to get ready? Nine more days would add up to forty: a full Lent. A 'butterfly Lent,' he thought. Or a pupal one. He truly liked the sound of those phrases. Who knew if those might eventually become the gateway to a new poem?

He pedaled on slowly, chasing the shade of rosewoods that caressed his nude shoulders.

A rider was awaiting him by the doorstep. Slowly, Guillermo rode his bike all the way to where the man stood. Oh, hello… He suddenly remembered him. As they scrutinized each other's faces, the chains of both bicycles almost became entangled. They smiled, carefully back-pedaled, and gave each other a funny look as things finally got settled.

"Do you remember me?"

"I certainly do," Guillermo responded. "How's everything going?"

"My grandson seems to be doing better these days."

"I'm glad to hear that."

"Take a look at these covers," the man said. "My wife knitted them for you."

By the time he entered the house, Guillermo was feeling like a different person. He headed towards the bathroom in order to wash his face. He left the tap running until the stream of water became *Tibet-cold*. Eventually, he found himself struggling to turn off the faucet.

It had been a minute since the last time he replaced the valve. He closed the stopcock and searched for a potentially lifesaving tutorial online. He dismissed the first two results, since the quality of the recordings was not the best. As for the third one, he was unable to comprehend the video without subtitles. The fourth result, however, came in quite handy, even though Guillermo would constantly get distracted—and somewhat concerned—by the bruises on the plumber's hands.

There were no spare valves in the toolbox. It was barely noon. Guillermo headed for the shed, grabbed his bike, and rode it to a nearby hardware store.

The place appeared crowded, although only four customers were inside. By noon, Guillermo had already entered the store. He examined the opening-hours sign, which listed 12:30 p.m. as the closing time. An electrician rested his elbows on the counter in a relaxed manner, showing no signs of being in a hurry. Soccer was broadcasting on TV. Guillermo decided to spend the wait examining the materials and accessories in the store. Was it wise to purchase a spare chain for his bike? How about gardening gloves? Or some wire mesh? Or even a new sprinkler? Once his turn came, Guillermo told the clerk about his incident with the faucet, hinting that he might need a replacement valve.

"Are you searching for a leather valve or a rubber one?"

"Rubber should work. Thanks."

It could well be an issue with the rod. Momentarily, Guillermo thought that he might not be able to shower for a few hours. The very possibility made him perspire profusely.

"I'll get one of those rods, too. Just in case."

On his ride back, Guillermo became increasingly warmer. That day appeared to be all about heat, heat, and more heat. "At least I have a pool!" he thought to himself, almost out loud.

As soon as he arrived home, Guillermo kicked off his shoes and headed straight for the swimming pool. He dived into the water, not even bothering to undress. He would soon regret this; still, the pleasure of those first dips was undeniable.

He then resurfaced from the water, took off all of his clothes except for his underwear, and air-dried his skin for a while, eventually heading for the shed in search of the necessary tools. He then entered his tiny changing room, got rid of his wet underpants, and changed into a pair of clean shorts.

Guillermo turned back his attention to the tutorial, then headed for the bathroom with the new valve and the rod—as well as a set of wrenches, some adjustable pliers, and a couple of screwdrivers.

He dedicated his heart and soul to the repair, following the steps from the tutorial like he was performing a ritual. He successfully dismantled all the parts involved. The old valve was seemingly stuck and damaged on its base. As the repair progressed, a number of tools went missing at some point. Using a set of tweezers, Guillermo managed to remove the damaged valve and replace it by the new one. A final check was all that was left. He turned the stopcock open, then the faucet. Everything now appeared to be working seamlessly, with no leaking or dripping in sight.

Guillermo felt a sense of accomplishment—along with abundant perspiration! He decided to take a shower. As the purifying water kept running through his body, something dawned on Guillermo—for the duration of the absorbing task, he was unable to think of Iris for a single second. He did not feel guilty (as Malva would say, "you don't actually *feel* guilty, but rather you *think* of yourself as guilty"). Rather, quite the opposite: his ideas felt collected; his body and mind, refreshed.

He had effectively devoted his whole self to replacing a faucet valve. After all, he thought, that must be all it takes to live in the present.

Guillermo left the shower and, using the steamy mirror as a writing surface, he wrote: "I AM THE WRITER OF THE FOLLOWING."

Then, he added:

> Dark lightnings
> Are showing off
> In the clear skies up above.

After running out of space on the mirror, he decided to switch to the nearby tiles:

> (Slices of bacon
> Deep into boiling oil).
> An opportunity to mend,
> Welding the broken pieces together.
> An opportunity to *heal*.

A golden opportunity for Guillermo to give his all to the task at hand.

TWENTY-NINE

Someone knocked on the front door. "*Hello*," a man's voice could be heard from the other side.

"*It's me—Cosme*," the unexpected visitor announced.

Guillermo tried not to curse.

"What's wrong, Cosme? I'm taking a shower."

"*What do you take me for, Guillermo?*" there was a silence that ended when a flock of birds started to chirp from the pine tree they called home. "*If you were actually taking a shower, you wouldn't be able to answer the door.*"

Guillermo started to sweat profusely, almost as much as when he had replaced the faucet valve earlier that day.

"Give me one sec—I'm on my way."

Guillermo threw on one of his favorite T-shirts— the one imprinted with an image of tennis player Roscoe Tanner, as well as the words "Palm Springs, 1978. Serving at 153 mph."

He then rushed to the door.

"Oh." Cosme said in surprise. "I was just passing by…"

"So, what's up?"

Cosme was holding what appeared to be an old picture.

"I was searching for a clipping from the *El Atlántico* newspaper," he emphasized this, "when I came across this picture."

"What does that have to do with me?"

"I decided to bring it your way, so you see I'm not holding a grudge…"

Guillermo stopped Cosme in his tracks, like he was playing a forehand volley at over 300 miles per hour.

"How dare you say you don't hold a grudge? You seem totally out of it. Just to jog your memory— you're the one that broke up the couple."

Cosme smiled sheepishly and zeroed in on the picture in his hand, gently touching it as if he intended to save it from oblivion.

"What's that picture you brought along?"

"It was taken at the *Hair* musical, back in the day."

Guillermo's first reaction was to loosen up his shoulders, which immediately ceased to feel tense. He stared at Cosme. That had to be a joke, no doubt about it. But it was not. The picture displayed a young Guillermo, cozily settled at the Teatro Argentino. That was back in 1971.

"There's only so much we can know about life," Cosme began to lecture. "All we rely on is our own experiences. *Live and learn*." Guillermo did not listen to the first part. The sight of the old picture kept shaking the foundations of his very own existence.

"The other day, you asked if I recalled ever attending that musical," Cosme clarified. "While I don't remember being there, I did have this among my pictures. And there you are..."

"You can keep it," Cosme added. Guillermo inquired about the identity of the young lady sitting next to him. Cosme replied that he did not have a clue.

"Nice T-shirt, by the way," Cosme concluded. "Did you know Sam Groth recently set a new record?"

IX

Manuel looked forward to taking Leticia back to Argentina. There, they would be treading on familiar ground, in places like Montserrat or Balvanera. Fever, however, was giving him no respite. He constantly felt like he was being grabbed from his shirt lapels, then thrown into a wall.

Now, he found himself playing with Leticia on the sidewalk. To be precise, they were not playing, but rather selling old issues of a number of magazines. Those dangled from a rope that hung between two trees. Leticia would typically reproach Manuel for his unwillingness to sell his Roy Rogers collection.

At the hospital, Manuel headed for the front desk. The receptionist looked at him in sympathy and encouraged him to shower, as she offered to assist with any potential needs. The white linen pants and orange shirt now resembled a battle flag. While it had whistle-clean stripes, other parts of the shirt appeared to have been buried for decades on end.

"We do also have a clothes bank for patients that are..." The receptionist somehow managed to cut herself short before uttering the word *needy*.

Far from being self-conscious in terms of his smell and looks, Manuel reiterated his request. He wondered what he could offer, also trying to remember what he had in his pockets. Not much—just a few leftover coins.

"Do you have health insurance?" "Yes, I do." What you can pay for at Ezeiza airport might well be of no use in Kathmandu. They suggested that he leave his brand-new wife in the East. The hospital received the visit of a well-reputed doctor, who was originally from Burkina Faso.

THIRTY

"I lost the *Hair* ticket."

"*Where was that?*"

"On the boulevard of oblivion."

"*The boulevard of oblivion?*" Iris inquired. "*Nothing comes to mind.*"

Now, Guillermo realized he had not made that much progress. He could feel his back staggering in zigzag.

"*I've changed quite a bit.*"

In Kathmandu, Iris' short concentration span would become known as 'the South American lady's evil.' She would become easily distracted, her mind resembling a grasshopper that jumps around. Ironically, the use of the phrase would have no *evil* associated, but typically emerged in a context of brotherhood.

"Well—who hasn't?" Guillermo replied. "I'm no longer the person I once was, either. Are you familiar with the concept of *apoptosis?*"

"*There seems to be a volcano over my eyes,*" Iris reflected out loud. Following a dull silence, she eventually burst into laughter.

At that point, Guillermo felt an irresistible urge to see her in mundanity, in everyday life questions like 'what are you wearing?' "I wish you could see my outfit right now," she would say. "I look like a cute tiny orange." "Here, everyone likes to dress like this." Iris then provided some clarification on something Guillermo might already have known at the time. In India, orange is associated with offenders and outlaws alike. At some point, beggars also began to wear orange as a way to display their marginalized status. That was also the case for Buddha, who sought to demonstrate his repudiation of a life filled with regal pleasures.

"It's so revealing that you've decided to bring up that musical," Iris resumed. *"This tunic clearly has some powerful New Age vibes. What about you? What are you wearing right now?"*

Guillermo mentioned he was wearing his run-of-the-mill tennis outfit, but insisted on learning more about Iris' life in Kathmandu. Therefore, she continued to talk:

"It was my fate to come here and fulfill the ritual."

At this point, Iris' voice resembled a soothing massage on Guillermo's ear.

"Are you still there?"

That feeling of reassuring yawn first thing in the morning.

"Here I am," Guillermo replied instantly.

Iris' words traveled through Guillermo's right ear, providing a quasi-mystical experience.

"I planned out the ritual all by myself."

That sight of something soft and fluffy, like the first bunny in one's childhood.

"*I headed for the top of the mountain and carefully chose the best patch of ice. I then returned to the valley. I placed the ice inside a clay jar, then worshipped it—keeping it safe until it eventually turned into water. Finally, I drank up the water.*"

Guillermo felt a warm light running down the arm he was using to hold the phone, eventually reaching his heart.

"That sounds seamless," he said.

"*That's the way the universe was conceived.*"

Guillermo was still holding the old picture taken at the Teatro Argentino.

"If I send you a picture, will you tell me the identity of whoever's sitting next to me?"

"*Sure. Right now?*"

"Yes. It's on its way."

The journey only lasted the time it takes for an instant message to travel from Argentina to Nepal. "Did you get it?" A silence ensued, like that of a grasshopper jumping around Kathmandu.

"Iris? Are you still there?" Guillermo insisted. "Did you recognize the girl sitting next to me?"

The black-and-white tones brightened up the image, turning the present day and those to come into sacred springs, the kind that Rainer M. Rilke would describe.

"*That's me,*" Iris said. "*The girl in the picture is me.*"

INDEX